Start Affiliate Marketing

Start Affiliate Marketing

ALSO BY SPENCER COFFMAN

A Guide To Deception
Relax And Unwind
Work Less Live More
A Healthier You!
Affiliate Marketing Expert
More Facebook Everything
365 Days Of Devotion For Everyone
YouTube Takeover
Find Us On Pinterest

Start Affiliate Marketing

START AFFILIATE MARKETING

How To Build Your Business
From The Ground Up

BY
SPENCER COFFMAN

Start Affiliate Marketing

While every precaution has been taken in the preparation of this book, the author and/or publisher assumes no responsibility for errors or omissions, or for damages resulting from the use of the information contained herein.

START AFFILIATE MARKETING: HOW TO BUILD YOUR BUSINESS FROM THE GROUND UP

First edition. April 2018.

ISBN: 978-1-9866696-0-3 (Paperback)
ISBN: 978-1-3869802-0-9 (Digital)

Copyright © 2018 by Spencer Coffman.
Cover Design by Spencer Coffman.
All Rights Reserved.

Written by Spencer Coffman.
SpencerCoffman.com

"Discover How To Build Your Business From The Ground Up"

Learn exactly how to start affiliate marketing and get rich by selling other people's products!

Virtually everyone in the workforce thinks about starting his or her own business at least once during his or her career. Those with entrepreneurial spirits think about it several times a month.

What's Stopping You?

One of the largest reasons people fail to follow their entrepreneurial dreams is a lack of capital. Or the false belief that they lack the proper capital.

YES, FALSE BELIEF

That's what so great about affiliate marketing. You can get started today without spending any money! Then, you can start building your business with extremely low costs.

In fact, it is possible to be an affiliate marketer without spending any money at all. However, many affiliate marketers choose to invest in their business because it makes things easier if you have the right tools.

Start Affiliate Marketing

You no doubt know what affiliate marketing is but just in case...

Affiliate marketing is the practice of selling other people's products and receiving a commission for selling those products.

People have made hundreds of millions of dollars all over the Internet simply by promoting other people's products. And now you can as well!

Living The Affiliate Life

The greatest advantage of being an affiliate marketer is that you can work from anywhere as long as you have an Internet connection.

You can take advantage of low-cost living in places like Mexico, The Bahamas, Thailand, or anywhere you like!

You can literally live in paradise while you build your business!

The point is, you can live wherever you want. You can work whenever you want. You are your own boss!

How to Get Started?

Becoming an affiliate marketer is pretty easy. However, being a successful affiliate marketer takes hard work and perseverance. You need to know what you are doing and make sure that what you are doing is going to be effective.

The last thing you want is to waste valuable time doing something that isn't going to work out.

You need a guide, a roadmap, a coach. You need someone to show you the ropes so you can see exactly what to do. Learn from someone else's mistakes instead of making your own. This will save you time and money.

Introducing:

Start Affiliate Marketing

You'll discover...

- What it takes to become an affiliate marketer

- How to earn money selling other people's products

- The best affiliate programs to join

- How to drive tons of traffic to your site

- Ways to promote other peoples products

- How to build your brand

Start Affiliate Marketing

- The most effective ways to build an online presence

- Exactly how to construct your business

- And Much Much More!

What Are You Waiting For!

It's obvious that affiliate marketing is one of the fastest ways to start making money online with little to no upfront costs.

It is said that wise people learn from the mistakes of others and foolish people forsake advice and make their own mistakes.

Which Type Of Person Are You?

Because this is an instant download, you can start learning how to become a successful affiliate marketer instantly!

Yes! I really want to learn how I can start making huge affiliate commissions online starting today!

So please send me my copy of "Start Affiliate Marketing" so I can build my online business and start making money selling other people's products right away!

Claim Your Copy Today!

Start Affiliate Marketing

Start Affiliate Marketing

Start Affiliate Marketing

Table of Contents

Introduction

Chapter 1: The Basics of Affiliate Marketing
    Does It Work
    Who Does It Benefit
    Why It May Not Work

Chapter 2: Choosing Your Niche And Market
    Your Target Market
    Every Niche Has A Market

Chapter 3: Getting Set Up
    Choosing Your Domain Name
    Web Hosting
    Building Your Website

Social Media

Chapter 4: SEO
Google Search Console
On Page SEO
Off Page SEO

Chapter 5: Marketing & Advertising
Video Marketing
Social Media Marketing
Email Marketing
Content Marketing
Creating Ads
Optimizing Ads

Chapter 6: Building A Brand
Target Your Market
Your Voice
Visual Branding
Brand Consistency

Chapter 7: Stick With It

Table of Contents

Make A Commitment
Stay Up To Date

Chapter 8: Conclusion

Appendix: Resources

Start Affiliate Marketing

Introduction

For many people out there, the ultimate goal is to achieve a passive income. Whether they are working to build a business of self-employment or are working for someone else with the intentions to receive a pension, everyone's goal is to make money while doing what they want to do. Everyone hopes to have a passive income. Whether it is now, or as a form of retirement in the future.

Although called "passive income" it isn't entirely passive. It is an income that requires little to no work to maintain. Notice the word maintain. It requires little to no work to maintain. However, it requires an immense amount of work to achieve. Achieving a passive income leads to a vast range of new opportunities where people can finally do what they want to do. Of course, that passive income needs to be high enough to pay for whatever they want to do. The point is that pretty much everyone has a goal of being retired yet still being able to make money.

This is the goal of being financially free. It means having all of your expenses paid while having the time and extra money to do anything you want to do. This means living within your means and not having to work a nine to five day job. It means saving money, not going into immense debt, and making smart choices. You'll have time to spend with your family and friends. You can take a vacation and if you want to stay a few extra days, no problem!

If given the chance to give up the nine to five day-to-day job and make money, most people would take it. Do you want to be able to retire now? Do you want to work for enjoyment rather than money to pay the bills that only keep coming back? Perhaps you would like to travel the world while the money rolls in while you sleep. In any case, a passive income is the key to all of this, and more!

The question becomes, how can one achieve a passive income? Well, there is the traditional way of working for a company for 20 to 40 years and receiving a pension. This is the method of the baby boomer generation. However, many companies no longer offer pension plans or provide retirements. Therefore, it is quickly becoming a method of the past.

There is also the method of working very hard for 20 to 40 years while investing your money in your own individual retirement account, or IRA. Then, after many years, your investments will, hopefully, have grown large enough that you will have the required amount of money you need to live the rest of your life without having to work for someone else. This starting to be the method of today's world, because if you don't save for your retirement, chances are, you are not going to get one.

Introduction

The third method is to start your own business and work very hard. You must invest in yourself. Not only in your business, but also in your education so you can learn how to properly run your business. This method requires a lot of time, work, and effort. You must build something from the ground up. You are building something and working very hard now so that you can sit back and watch it grow later.

With all of the Internet opportunities today, this method is becoming increasingly popular among the millennial generation. They are becoming affiliate marketers, online entrepreneurs, YouTube sensations, bloggers, and anything that has to do with making money on the Internet. They are plugged in doing things that their parents and grandparents don't even understand. Yet, they are making money and lots of it.

Depending on your understanding, this may seem easy or difficult. However, no matter how it seems right now, it is not what you think. If you think it is going to be a walk in the park then you are in for a rude awakening. It is going to be hard work. On the other hand, if you think it is going to be too difficult. Then you are in for a pleasant surprise because it won't be as hard as you think. Affiliate marketing is a solid approach and if you learn what to do, then doing it will come easy.

Building a business can be done quickly and easily if you know what you are doing. It is learning what to do that makes things difficult. It is sticking with it and working when everyone else is out having fun. Sacrifice. You

Start Affiliate Marketing

must set goals and know that you are working toward a better future. You are building something that will last for generations and provide an income for your children and your children's children. Sure, you may not see immediate benefits. However, someday you'll have something that you can leave behind and know that everyone is taken care of.

Think about how online shopping has changed the world. If you want a toothbrush, Amazon will bring it to your door in two days. You want a 50-pound bag of pet food? No problem, with only a few clicks, Amazon delivers. It isn't only Amazon. How about sifting through craft shows to find cool things that you can have? Etsy has it all in one place. Looking for antiques, collectibles, or anything really? eBay is the place for you. The list goes on!

All of these places make tons of money by having other people buy and sell things on their websites. Then, tons of other people make money by helping those sites get more sales. Those people drive traffic to the sites and get other people to purchase products. They don't have to do any shipping, any product listing, any buying, nothing. All they have to do is refer someone to make a purchase on that website. They are affiliate marketers.

This is what you are going to do. You are going to start making money by referring other people to purchase products that are not yours. This means you don't have to do anything except marketing. In doing so, you are helping several people accomplish their goals. This is why affiliate marketing is so amazing. You help

Introduction

the seller of the product make a sale. You help the buyer of the product find exactly what he or she was looking for. You help the platform grow. And, you help yourself.

You are about to vastly increase your knowledge of not only affiliate marketing, but also building a successful online business in general. You'll learn how to get started as an affiliate marketer. Including all of the necessary setup, equipment, hosting, et cetera. You'll learn about starting a website, social media accounts, blogs, and other online networking activities. You'll learn how to optimize all of that information so people will be able to find your links. In addition, you will do all of this on autopilot so you don't have to be a slave that constantly is keeping up with posting to 100 different places several times a day!

You'll also learn a lot about business and marketing. You are going to build a strong brand. You'll advertise with success and begin earning a passive income by selling other people's products with very little start-up costs. Then, eventually, you will start earning enough money so you won't have to work as hard. You can hire some help and sit back while the money continues rolling in day after day.

However, there is one thing that you must understand before starting any of this. It is a very important point and you need to be ready for what is about to happen. You cannot expect to earn a completely passive income. In fact, you will always have to do some work. As time goes on, it may only be a few hours a week. It may even be paying someone to do all of that work for you. The bottom line is that you will always have to maintain your business. Only so much can be done on autopilot. There still needs to be some human element to keep things going.

In addition, you are not going to become wildly rich right away. You are building a business. That means it is going to take some time. You are going to have to work during nights and weekends to get the foundations laid. You are not building a house you are building a skyscraper. That means it will take some time. Affiliate marketing often starts off slowly and then grows all of a sudden. There will be a tipping point. Once you get that snowball to the top of the mountain and give it that final push. It will roll down the other side and continually grow bigger and bigger.

How long it takes to get that snowball to the top of the mountain depends on how much valuable effort you put into your business. I say valuable effort because sometimes people work very very hard but they are working in the wrong direction. They may be going around the mountain instead of up it. This is why you need to educate yourself so that you aren't merely spinning your wheels. You need to know what you are doing and exactly what you are going to get out of doing it.

You will make money selling other people's products and it is essential that you are willing to put in the time and effort. Like any real business, you are not going to get rich quick. This isn't some scheme. It is a business. You can build it and succeed. Affiliate marketing is becoming more and more popular and nearly every

Introduction

online vendor has an affiliate program. Therefore, use this book to learn all you can about affiliate marketing. Then, take a look at my other books because many of them can help you with your business as well.

Stick with it, never give up, and you will most definitely succeed.

Start Affiliate Marketing

Chapter 1:

The Basics of Affiliate Marketing

One of the most popular ways to make money online today is affiliate marketing. This is because of the ease and simplicity that it provides. You don't have to worry about being home all of the time so that you can send out a product when it sells. You don't need a budget to purchase your inventory and other supplies. In addition, you don't need to have space for inventory, packing materials, et cetera. All you need is a computer, an Internet connection, and a few hundred dollars of start-up money. That's it!

But first, what is affiliate marketing? Well, in case you

Start Affiliate Marketing

are unfamiliar, affiliate marketing is a great way to make money by promoting other people products or services so that people buy them. You are referring customers to a certain place and when those customers make a purchase you earn a commission on the sale. You are sort of like a salesman for that company. You are an outside salesman working on an external commission.

The amount of money you make varies on how many people you get to make a purchase. The more people that buy things, the more commission you make. Therefore, your goal is to refer as many people as possible to the products or services you are promoting. You are now in the sales and marketing business. You are working for straight commission and since you can automatically be employed with any of the companies that sell products, there is a lot of money to be made.

You don't have to worry about non-compete clauses or promoting similar products from companies that are competitors to one another. In fact, you can market the same product on both Amazon and eBay. In fact, it is even encouraged! Why would you do this? Because some people are loyal to certain places. They may have Amazon prime so they'll pay a little more to buy it on Amazon instead of eBay so they can get their free two-day shipping. Or, they may be loyal to eBay because they like paying with PayPal.

There are a variety of reasons your buyers will choose one outlet over another. Therefore, if you can offer several of the main outlets then your chances of getting someone to click on your link are significantly increased. In addition, you can easily capture all of these markets because you can be an affiliate for any company that has an affiliate program!

Does It Work?

Short answer, yes. Of course, it works. There are many people who have become very successful in the world of affiliate marketing. There are also those who shoot videos from their private yachts, so they claim, about how much money they are making. The world is filled with all sorts of people. There are those that try to scam you, there are those that lie about their success, there are those that are sincere, and there are those that fall for all the lies. Which person are you?

If you've been searching for a way to make money online then this is it. You can work at your own pace and only you control your destiny. You are the sole proprietor of your success. You've no doubt come across many business ideas or plans for success. You may have even tried several of them and been disappointed. You've probably been skeptical about many others because they promise the moon or perhaps they charge large sums of money and claim that it is an investment.

If you are struggling, wondering where to turn and how to get started then know this. You can do everything on your own for very low amounts of money. The good news is that you will make money with affiliate marketing. Affiliate marketing is a real thing and it works. There are no costs to join affiliate programs and you can start promoting products right now. You could make your first sale in minutes. All it takes is a social media post and for someone to click on it.

There are tons of ways for you to promote products and that means tons of ways for you to make sales. It is a process of which you are in complete control. It's all you. Therefore, if you want to work really hard and start making large amounts of money fairly quickly then you will! If you want to do it on the side and build your business over time then it will happen! You're the boss. The good news is that affiliate marketing works and if you work for it, then it will work for you.

Who Does It Benefit?

Affiliate marketing is a great thing for a variety of different people. Not only will you be benefiting yourself by earning a commission on the sale, but you will also benefit the seller of the product, the customer, and the platform. It's a direct win-win-win-win situation that will benefit even more than those four main parties. Think about all of the other people who benefit. The manufactuer, the shipping service, the packing material companies, the Internet hosting and server companies, the list goes on! However, there are four main people that benefit anytime you make a sale. They are the customer, the seller, the platform, and yourself.

The Customer
When you refer a customer to a product, you are putting them in touch with the product that they have been searching for. You are filling a need that

they had. You are going to help this customer with something that they needed help with. Whatever product they are purchasing at your recommendation is going to make their life easier or help them in some way. Therefore, they are benefiting from your affiliate marketing efforts.

The Seller
The seller of the product is benefitting from your affiliate marketing efforts because he or she has received a sale. This is their purpose for putting products online. They want to sell them. When you get someone to make a purchase, the seller has successfully reached his or her goal of selling a product and makes money doing so. If you can refer several buyers then the seller will really start doing well and may not even know why.

In addition, their reputation and status will be increased due to the sales you are providing them. They will also be building their brand through your referrals. They have gained a customer who may not have found their product if it weren't for you. Not only that, but the seller didn't have to pay you to market their product. That means they received some amazing free advertising that you provided them. This is a very huge benefit for them.

The Platform
If the seller is not paying you a commission on the sale then who is? The platform. Why would they do this? They know that by getting you to promote products on their platform they will get more people to visit the platform. That means they will increase

their brand recognition. In addition, they may also get some more sales out of the deal. If you refer someone for a specific product, that person may shop around for other products. Thereby giving the platform even more business.

They can afford to pay you a commission because if sellers know that they are dedicating large amounts of money to help them succeed then they will continue selling on that platform. That means the platform will make more money because the more money the sellers make the more money the platform makes. Whenever a product is sold online, the platform earns a commission of the sale. It is a fee that the seller of the product must pay. Not only that, but sellers who are doing well will often pay the platform a membership fee to help promote their products.

Therefore, if the platform can get you to help bring them more traffic, then they will do better overall. Sure, they may have to pay you a little bit up front. However, in the end, they will end up making even more money because they have helped a seller be more successful. Not only that, but they have also gained a customer that they can market to and get even more sales on their own without having to pay a commission.

You
Not only do you help all of those other people succeed, you'll help yourself succeed as well. Your business will grow when you refer people to good products. Chances are that they will continue to visit your website for more great deals. Thus, you will

build your brand, recognition, and a loyal customer base. Not only that, you will also be earning money in the process. The more referrals you make the more money you will earn!

If you can continually refer people to great products then you will continue to earn great affiliate commissions. In addition, as you build your business, you will start getting people to visit your website that you didn't even market to. That means you will begin earning money at all hours of the day, even when you're sleeping! This is the start of a true recurring income that is on its way to becoming more and more passive.

Why It May Not Work

The fastest way to start affiliate marketing is to begin signing up for affiliate programs on a variety of websites. You can sign up on Amazon, eBay, Overstock, Clickbank, Commission Junction, et cetera. Then, simply start promoting products. You can promote products by sharing them on your social media, your website, blog, et cetera.

Many affiliate marketers begin this way. They start promoting a variety of products from a variety of places and then wonder why they are not making very many sales. They continually share products and practically spam their social media accounts hoping that people will click on these products and purchase them. They are shooting in the dark with a shotgun hoping that their wide pattern will hit something.

Start Affiliate Marketing

If you are currently affiliate marketing in this manner then push the pause button until you finish this book because you need to do some restructuring. However, if it is working for you then, obviously, let it continue working for you. Chances are, it isn't. The reason is that there is no direction. There is no plan of attack. You need structure and a valid approach if you are going to succeed.

In order to be successful with affiliate marketing, there needs to be a clear and concise plan of action. This also needs to be apparent to anyone that comes across your business. They need to have an idea of who you are and what you are doing. You don't need to tell them your plan but they should be able to see what you are doing simply through encountering your business. It should be readily apparent but not broadcasted.

They should be able to see exactly what you are selling so that they know anytime they need products related to your niche that they can count on you to provide them with a good recommendation. Therefore, before you go crazy trying become a successful affiliate marketer, take some time to lay the foundation. There are several steps to learn and many details that should be ironed out before you begin.

This is why it is very important for you to choose a niche before you start doing any sort of promotion. You need to know and understand what you are going to be promoting. This way, you will be able to target groups of people and, as a result, you'll have a much higher success rate.

Chapter 2:

Choosing Your Niche And Market

The very first step when it comes to any form of online marketing business is to choose your niche. This is very important because you need to know beforehand what you are going to promote. This should be done before you do anything else. You need to have a clear direction of what you are going to do and how you are going to get there. After all, if you don't know where you are going you'll never arrive.

That being said, selecting the right products or services to market can be a very overwhelming task. There are so many different options and finding the right one for you may seem like a never-ending battle. However, don't let it get to you. Often times, you already know exactly what you want to promote. If you don't consciously know, then it is unconscious. You simply have never thought about it before. Therefore, take some time to think about it and use the following paragraphs to guide your thoughts.

Avoid trying to promote products simply because they are expensive. Stay away from promoting products because they are popular. Don't promote products for the sole reason of earning a higher commission. If you focus on the money then you're going the wrong direction. You need to promote products because you genuinely believe they are a good product or service and you want to share them with others. Doing this will help your business in many ways.

If you promote things that you are interested in and would use yourself, then you will have a much better time doing so than if you promote things based on the money. You'll also be a lot more believable when telling others about the products. The first rule of being in business for yourself is to enjoy what you do. After all, why on earth would you become self-employed if you don't like your job? If you don't like it, then do something else! You're the boss!

Many affiliate marketers choose products that are already selling well. Although this can be good in theory, it usually causes a lot of trouble. First, you may not know about these products. Second, because they are selling well, that means there is a lot of competition. In addition, if they are already selling

Choosing Your Niche And Market

well that means the platform is going to be promoting them. Do you really want to compete with a platform like Amazon? You'll lose.

This is why choosing a niche is so important when it comes to sales. If your visitors see that you are promoting all kinds of unrelated products then they will not be as loyal. Your business will seem less structured. It will appear random and chaotic. It will also be more work for you to keep everything organized. Your customers may become confused as to what you are really doing, which will end up driving them away.

You need to be able to offer specific products to your customer base. They need to know that they can always count on you to provide XYZ. This will greatly increase your credibility and brand recognition. Work to achieve consistency and promote related products or services. If you do this, then your customers will be much more likely to share your content and return to your business in the future. They will be able to know that the products you promote will be directly related to their interests. That will make them loyal followers of your brand.

Therefore, find a good niche that you are interested in and that encompasses a variety of products. If you choose a broad niche with a lot of sub-niches then you will be able to promote many products and services that are all related to your main niche. This will help build your business and establish your credibility. You will look reliable, consistent, and trustworthy. This is because your visitors will be able to see that you have a direction and a purpose.

One of the largest questions affiliate marketers have when starting out is whether they should promote expensive products or inexpensive products. It is a mistake to think that one or the other will make more money. However, many people reason that expensive products will earn more because they are more expensive. Other people reason that inexpensive products will earn more because more people can afford them.

If you are selling several $10 items and your commission is five percent then you are not going to make very much per sale. However, if your target market has millions of people then you will probably do just fine. On the other hand, if you are promoting items that cost $500 and your commission is five percent then you will make a good amount per sale. However, if your target market only has a few thousand people then you may have some trouble continually selling those products.

Basically, the price of the products or services you promote is a minor factor in your success. The price isn't going to significantly determine whether or not you will earn a lot of money. The major factor in your success is finding the right people to purchase the products or services that you are going to promote. If you can find the right people then you will be successful. Remember that there are already tons of people out there buying the products you plan to promote. Now, you simply need to get them to buy them through you.

Choosing Your Niche And Market

Your Target Market

After you have selected a niche, you need to find your target market. You need to determine your intended customers and find out who would be most likely to buy the products you promote. One important thing is that finding your target market can also help you find your niche. This will mean opening up your mind to some different stereotypes. However, the thing to remember in marketing is that stereotypes often hold true. This is why they were created, to better market to certain types of people. Marketing is one huge stereotype so get used to it.

For example, if you are going to sell baby strollers then you are going to market to parents, probably mothers, who have little children. This means you need to specifically target women, not men. Another example that is a little more direct would be if you were going to promote hair combs. Your target market would primarily be men because women don't usually use combs they use brushes. In addition, you would probably not market to black men because they will most likely use a hair pick.

Take that scenario and switch it around in any way you like. Maybe you are promoting all kinds of hair grooming products. You would not try to sell a hair pick to a white woman with long straight hair, would you? Would you try to sell a hairbrush to a man with a crew cut? If you do then you won't be in business very long because they aren't going to buy it. Therefore, pay attention to different marketing stereotypes and use them to help you promote products to targeted groups of people.

Basically, the point is that choosing your niche and target market go hand in hand with each other. You need to think in black and white terms and use stereotypes. Yes, they may be controversial but they work when it comes to sales. You are going to profile and generalize anyone who needs the specific products you are promoting.

Anyone with hair will use some form of hair groomer. If they are women that means a hairbrush, most men use combs, and black people use hair picks. It's really simple. Although this isn't always the case, it is generally true. It is a stereotype. Therefore, use them to your advantage to market certain products to certain types of people and increase the possibility of sales.

Every Niche Has A Market

It is important for you to understand that every niche has a market and vice versa. No matter what you want to promote there is someone out there that wants to purchase that product. Whether you choose a large niche like online gambling or a smaller niche like diamond tipped arrowheads there is a market for all of them. The main thing is that you need to choose a niche that has a variety of niches within it.

Therefore, if you are really excited to promote diamond tipped arrowheads then you probably want to make arrows your niche. That means you'll promote

Choosing Your Niche And Market

all kinds of different arrowheads from target to big game. You could even widen your niche and promote arrows as well. The point here is that you shouldn't get stuck with one small narrow niche. Give yourself some room to maneuver.

Start by listing the products and services that interest you. Chances are that there will be more than you think. List your hobbies, the services you pay for on a monthly basis, your passions, et cetera. Do you love video games, beauty products, or watching TV? Do you subscribe to Netflix, Hulu, Amazon Prime, or any other club-based subscription service? If you are interested in the products you are going to promote then you will be a much more effective promoter and people will buy from you.

If you are having a hard time finding your niche and target market then use these questions to help you find your ideal customers. They will help you see things from their point of view so you can put yourself in the shoes of your audience. This will help you better understand your customers and what you would like to sell them.

Even if you have already found your niche and audience it would still be a good idea for you to read through the questions. Use them to help you refine and better understand your audience. After all, the more you can target your audience the better you will be able to meet their needs and communicate with them. That means you will have better chances of making sales and your business will have a better chance of success.

Start Affiliate Marketing

These questions will get you to focus on three main areas of your marketing efforts. The first is the people. You need to know and understand your people. Second is information. You need to know and understand what information you are going to deal with. The third is your competitors. You need to know your competitors and what they are doing. This will help you stay sharp and up to date.

What kind of people are you trying to reach?
You probably already know what type of people use, or need, the products or services you are promoting. However, you may not have thought about it yet. They are the people who use the product or service and who continually purchase it. You may or may not know and interact with these people. However, you know of them and you can easily find out what they are in to based on their social media activity.

For example, if these people purchase a lot of workout DVD's and exercise products then you will know that you are trying to reach health-conscious people. They will most likely not be interested in gym memberships because they have purchased all of the stuff to use at home. That means they will probably be interested in fitness gear, health food products, other work out programs, et cetera. Use your powers of logic, reasoning, and deduction to understand how these people operate.

You need to find out what types of people are constantly spending money in your niche and you need to target them. This will help you know what to promote and when to promote it. It will also help you make sure you aren't constantly promoting something that they already have. If you know what they are buying then you can promote related products that they will be likely to purchase. Fortunately, Facebook can help you find all of this information using their ads research tools.

What do these people look like?
Are you marketing to a scrawny beanpole that needs some protein shakes? Or are you marketing to a big fat person that needs to lose weight? Are they male or female? How old are they? Consider the demographic information of your target market. What does your ideal customer look like? Bring out all of those stereotypes and think about them. In many cases, sales stereotypes hold true so start using them to your advantage.

Paying attention to this information will help you determine what types of products they will like. If they are bulked up guys with spiky hair then they probably aren't going to be in the market doomsday survival gear. They will probably be looking for sweatpants, blender bottles, muscle enhancing products, et cetera. On the other hand, those doomsday survival people may like your diamond tipped arrowheads because then they'll be able to take down any foe that tries to steal their food.

Of course, there is always the possibility that someone may be shopping for someone else. In that case, they will buy something that they may not normally buy. These are outliers and should be thrown out of your data pool. The reason is that this behavior is not consistent and you should not let it skew your marketing research.

Where are these people from?
Knowing where these people are from is similar to their demographical information. However, this is more focused on where they came from rather than where they are living. It is their heritage. It's their roots. Think about the heritage of the people who use the products you are going to promote and apply some stereotypes.

The stereotypes you want to consider are heritage-based stereotypes. That means they may not be politically correct to discuss but they hold true nonetheless. Things like: Asian people are shorter, black people are more athletic, white Americans spend more money, et cetera. Remember that when it comes to sales, the stereotypes often times hold true. Therefore, use them to market to these people.

In addition, think about where these people are currently living. If they are living in the middle of a big city then you will market differently than if they are living in the suburbs or in the county. If your target audience lives in the city then you are probably not going to sell them tools for farming. You are going to sell them things for indoor and patio plants because that is what they can use.

What are they looking for?
Think about the goals of your audience. What do they hope to gain by purchasing the products you are

promoting? If a big fat person purchases some diet books then it is pretty obvious that the end goal is to lose weight. However, it isn't always this easy. Still, you can very easily make some general determinations by thinking about what the product or service is designed to do. Do you use it? If so, what do you use it for? Chances are the result of that product will be the end goal of the customer.

Is this product a necessity or is it a luxury item or want. This will tell you whether or not they will purchase it to serve a specific purpose, like purchasing a tool, or whether it is something that they purchase to make them happy. Is it an impulse buy that gives instant gratification or something else? Determine what problems the product solves. If you know what they hope to accomplish then you will be much better able to sell to them by marketing to their emotions and satisfying that desire.

You need to market to their emotions. People don't buy anything simply for the sake of buying it. In addition, most people are not practical when it comes to making purchases. It's not a thought process. They buy things to make them feel better or to remove some form of pain or problem in their life. Looks like Freud was right, we are all motivated to seek pleasure and avoid pain. Use the pleasure that the product provides or the problem it relieves as a marketing tactic to get more sales.

What kind of information do they want to know?
You know the needs of your audience and what they are looking for. Therefore, what kind of additional

information would interest them? Is there anything that would help them? Think of some additional ways of pleasing your customers. You won't make money on this. It will be done solely for the purpose of providing useful information to them. It will help you build trust and keep them loyal to your business.

If you can provide them with additional information then they will be more apt to return to your blog, website, profile, et cetera. This will help you because you want them to come back so they can see what else you are promoting. The more they come back the more likely they'll click on another one of your affiliate links. People like it when other people help them. They don't want to be constantly sold to so if you take care of, and support, them then they will be happy to occasionally support you. Notice I said occasionally, they will not always click on your links. However, they will if you have something they need or want.

Would they be willing to pay for this information?
Once you know what information they want, you need to decide if it is worth it to charge them for this information. Is it worth selling? If so, how much would they be willing to pay you for it? Are you going to sell it as a subscription or a one-time purchase? How will you deliver this information? Text, email, online login, et cetera. You need to decide if you want to offer this information as a free service to your customers or if it is worth it for you to try and sell it to them in addition to promoting products.

Keep in mind that you are already trying to get them to click on the products you are promoting so they will

Choosing Your Niche And Market

buy the product through your affiliate link. Therefore, adding additional information for them to pay for may not work out so well. Often times, the most successful businesses are those that put the needs of the customer first.

If you are constantly hounding them to try and make a sale, they probably won't stick around very long. On the other hand, if you are consistently providing them with good information that they can use, then they are going to like you for a long time. Remember, focus on your customers and the money will follow.

How do they want to get the content?
How will people receive and use the products or services that you promote? Are you selling material that will be available online or is it something that will be physically sent to them in the mail? Is it video, audio, or text-based? This may seem trivial but it is important because not all people can use all of these formats. Think about people with disabilities or certain learning styles. A blind person will never watch workout DVD's, however, they may listen to workout tips and ideas.

In addition, those who put in a lot of time behind the wheel may not read books. However, they may listen to your audiobooks or podcasts. Knowing the answer to this question is a large part of knowing your audience. If you know what your audience likes then you can promote products that specifically meet their needs.

Companies like AmazonFresh, Blue Apron, and other food delivery subscription services have this figured out. They know that their target audience doesn't like to go shopping or plan meals. They also know that they have money and like the convenience of home delivery. Another stereotype in action. Therefore, they send the food right to their door and cater to those desires. All you have to do is make sure that the products you promote and your target market go hand in hand.

What are you doing for them?
What are you doing for the people that visit your business? Are you providing them with a review of the products or services? Do you give them free information? Are you providing them with discounts and other coupons? You must be doing something for them or they wouldn't be visiting your business and clicking on your links. If you aren't getting anyone clicking on your links then you must not be doing enough for your audience. Thus, you need to do more.

Do some research on your competitors and find out what other affiliate marketers are doing for their customers. See if they are providing any additional value other than a link to a product. Find out why people are clicking on their links rather than simply going directly to the platform itself. If you can find out how other affiliate marketers in your niche are getting clicks then you can use that to help you get clicks as well.

One thing that may be helpful is if you show people how it works, not tell them how it works. This is where the practicality of your niche comes into play. Are you looking to target the practical solution and results-based buyers or are you going after the buyers who make purchases on a whim? Decide who is going to purchase it and show them what it will do for them.

What are your competitors doing for them?
In order to answer this question, you need to have a niche in mind. Think of a niche and then start to see who your competitors would be. Then take a look at what they are offering to your target market. This is going to require a lot of research and investigation on your part and it is something that will continue even after you are in business. Knowing what your competitors are doing will greatly help your marketing efforts. Learn from them and mirror their campaigns.

Remember the saying "dress to be the person you want to be"? This is the same with your affiliate marketing competitors. Find someone who is promoting products in your niche and make an effort to be like them. Don't steal their methods but use them to shape your own. Remember that not all affiliate marketers are your competitors only those that are in the same niche as you. Therefore, consider teaming up with some other marketers who aren't in your niche.

Can you offer something better than your competitors?
Once you learn what your niche-competitors are doing to get people to click on their links, you can do the same thing with a few personal touches. Learn from what they are doing and make it better. Use their format and layout to market your products. You are copying their method of marketing, not the content

itself. In addition, see if you can find out something that your competitors are not doing and do it yourself.

Think about your niche and target market and see if there is anything else that would be helpful. People who have already purchased the products in your niche are great sources of information. Check out product reviews, social media pages, chat forums, et cetera to find out all you can about the things that people are complaining about. Then see if you can help provide solutions to those problems. Chances are there will be a lot of great feedback that you can use to meet the demands of this target market. It will take some time but it will be highly worthwhile.

Finishing Up
Knowing the answers to these questions will really help you discover your niche and find your target market. When you do that, you will be able to promote specific products to specific groups of people and you'll know that they are interested in them. Use these questions to help build your audience and drive more sales through your affiliate links.

Chapter 3:

Getting Set Up

Once you have chosen your niche and found your target market, you need to start signing up with different platforms that sell those types of products. Applying to be an affiliate is a very easy process that takes a small amount of time. Once you apply, you'll have to wait to be approved. Then, when you are approved, spend some time going over the terms and conditions of that platform. Learn the rules of affiliate marketing. This is very important because if you fail to follow certain rules on certain platforms then your affiliate status could be taken away.

If you wish to promote physical products start with places like Amazon, eBay, Overstock, Commission

Start Affiliate Marketing

Junction, and ClickBank. If you wish to sell digital products then JVZoo, Warrior Plus, Share-a-Sale, as well as Commission Junction and ClickBank will be good places to start. In addition, there are many other niche-specific websites out there that offer affiliate programs. Basically, find out who is selling the products you want to promote and then apply to be an affiliate on that platform.

It is also a good idea to find other platforms that sell the same, or similar, products. This way you can offer a variety of options to your customers. As mentioned earlier, some people are loyal to specific platforms. Therefore, if you can provide links to the same product on several platforms then you will be more likely to get a sale. However, you must be careful not to provide too many links. You don't want to overwhelm your visitors or make it confusing to them. Keep it simple and stick with the main platforms. This will provide credibility, legitimacy, and ease of use.

After you are approved on the appropriate platforms, it is time for you to start building your business. You need to decide how you are going to promote these products and set up a base of operations. This means you need a website. You need a place to post all of your product reviews, testimonials, information, or whatever content you are providing your customers to get them to click on your affiliate links.

Websites can be made on all sorts of different platforms. You can opt for a "real" website that uses your own domain name or you can use one of the free blog services like Blogger or WordPress. However, the

Getting Set Up

best option would be to use your own domain name and build a website that you can use to promote products. Then you can share all of your posts to your various social media accounts including Blogger and WordPress blogs. This will give your domain more authority and better SEO.

Choosing Your Domain Name

You can purchase your domain name on any number of different places. The most popular place is probably GoDaddy. They offer some great deals and you can buy domains at a pretty good price. One thing to keep in mind is that you will have to renew your domain name each year. Often times this may be at a higher price. Therefore, it may be a good idea for you to buy your domain for several years at a time.

There are some places out there that offer free yearly renewals, or lifetime domains. If you choose one of these places, make sure to find out if there are any requirements you have to meet in order to keep that benefit. Then find out if it is worth it for you to do so. Some places may require you to pay monthly or use their over-priced hosting service. Therefore, be sure to look into the details before making a purchase.

When selecting a name, it is important to choose one that is both easy to remember and easy to spell. It should be something that sticks in people's heads. You want them to be able to use it in conversation without having to specify how it is written. Avoid using hyphens or any strange characters. Basically, keep it simple.

Start Affiliate Marketing

For example, if you are promoting boards that get pulled behind a boat like wakeboards, kneeboards, wake surfboards, et cetera and name your business wakeryder then you are asking for trouble. Since rider is normally spelled with an "I" then anytime someone talks about your website they will have to say rider with a "Y". This may seem cool at first, but it will end up hurting your business because most people will spell rider with an "I".

You want your domain name to be niche-specific. That means it needs to be related to your niche. People should be able to instantly tell what your business is about based on the name you choose. If you are selling camping gear then you might choose bestcampgear.com as your domain name. Whatever your niche, make sure your domain name directly corresponds to the products and services you are promoting.

In addition, whatever name you choose will be your business name as well as your domain name. You'll also use that name across all of your social media accounts. In some cases, the name may not be available. If that happens, then simply add a number to the end. As long as you use the same or very a similar, pattern across all platforms you will be fine.

When selecting a domain name, it would be better for you to choose a dot-com domain. Nowadays you can find domain names with all kinds of dot extensions. However, dot-coms are still the most widely known and thought about domains. They are easier to remember because many people still assume that

Getting Set Up

dot-coms are the only domains out there for private use. It is what people are used to. Therefore, if at all possible, get a dot-com domain name.

Web Hosting

After you purchase your domain name, you will need to use some form of hosting service to get your website online. There are many different hosting providers and even more forms of hosting available. As a result, choosing the right one for your business can be very frustrating. You can drive yourself crazy with all of the options and various costs with each option.

The best thing to do is to select a reputable, big-name, hosting provider that has good support. When you are getting started, the last thing you want to have happen is technical problems. Therefore, spend a little more money to have good support and backup services. Usually, this is only $10 more a month. It's worth it. Unless you are a web hosting developer whiz, you should really budget for a good hosting provider.

Of course, there are some free hosting options out there. You can link your domain to a WordPress or Blogger blog. You can also use some sales funnel services that can link your domain. Whatever you choose, it is up to you. Here are some of the main hosting packages that will be available to you within each hosting provider.

Shared Hosting
This is one of the cheaper options on the market. Shared hosting means you will be sharing the hosting

server and resources with a number of other people. You'll all have the same servers and IP address. You will likely have certain limits on your account and if you exceed these limits your hosting may be suspended until you fall back within the limits. That means your site will be shut down until you fix the problem.

Shared hosting packages can be good if you purchase them with a fast hosting provider. A2 and GoDaddy are both pretty good. Avoid HostGator it is terribly slow and their support is awful. When you are on a shared hosting package, make sure you are watching the resource usage in your CPanel so you don't accidentally hit the limits. It's also a good idea to continually contact support so you develop a good relationship. That way they'll be able to help you out if you do get suspended.

One caution about shared hosting is that if someone on your hosting plan gets blacklisted or sandboxed then your site will lose rank. In other words, if another person whose website is on your server does some shady things, then the bots will simply flag the entire IP address. Since you share that IP, you can get hurt even though you didn't do anything wrong. Blacklisted and Sandboxed are terms used when a site is flagged for spamming and gets booted out of the search results.

This could also happen with your email deliverability. If someone on your shared hosting plan is continually sending out spam emails then your email deliverability may decrease. This is because you are sending emails from the same server they are. Thus, your email may be associated with the spam flag. Thus, if you notice

Getting Set Up

your emails are not going through then this could be what is going on.

For these reasons, you must constantly pay attention to your shared hosting details. Make sure you know your IP and server identity. Find out how everything works by contacting support and see what they are doing to help protect you against these things. You can also find different services online that will tell you what other sites share your IP address. I recommend running these searches and taking a look at the websites. If any of them appear shady then contact your hosting provider and see if you can be moved to a different server.

VPS Hosting
VPS hosting stands for Virtual Private Server. This means that you are still on a shared hosting account but your servers and IP mimic a dedicated hosting plan. Thus, you will essentially have your own server but you are still sharing resources with other people. If you hit the limits, your hosting account will still be suspended. But you won't have to worry about other people ruining your ranking due to their poor choices.

VPS hosting can be an excellent choice for people who want the peace of mind that comes with dedicated hosting without having to pay the premium prices. You don't have to worry about someone hurting your search ranking, email deliverability, et cetera. You are in complete control because you are, essentially, the only person on the server.

Support is pretty good with VPS hosting but they

will assume you know more than if you merely have a shared hosting plan. This can be a good and a bad thing. Sometimes you may not understand what they are talking about and other times you will be thankful that they are giving you a technical answer rather than a generic response. The main point is that as long as you choose a hosting provider with good support they will always help you no matter what plan you select.

Dedicated Hosting
Dedicated hosting is better than shared hosting and is one step above VPS hosting. Naturally, it is also more expensive. This is because instead of sharing resources, and cost, with other users you have the server all to yourself. Thus, you have to pay more. Dedicated hosting is good because you are in complete control of everything. You don't have to worry about another user causing problems for your website, search ranking, email deliverability, et cetera. You are the only one on the plan.

You do need to have more extensive knowledge of how hosting works if you use a dedicated server because support is usually less user-friendly. This means that they automatically assume that you know what you are doing. Therefore, they tend to give you more complex and advanced answers. That being said, if you are not advanced don't worry. Support will still help you out you'll simply have to explain your needs in a little more detail.

Cloud Hosting
Cloud hosting is different from traditional hosting in that everything is in the cloud. Rather than having

Getting Set Up

the information stored on servers in a warehouse somewhere it is all virtual. This can be a good thing for people who worry about servers crashing. It can also be a high risk if you are worried about something happening to the cloud.

Within cloud hosting, there are multiple packages that resemble the packages of traditional web hosting. You can have public cloud hosting, which means you share resources with other cloud users. Or you can have private cloud hosting, which means you have your own resources in the cloud.

One huge advantage of cloud hosting is that all of your information is stored on multiple virtual servers. This means that even if you share the hosting plan with multiple people there will be little chance of server overload. That means there will be less chance of your site getting shut down due to resource usage. Speed may also improve because the servers are virtual. So no matter where someone is when they get on your site, the distance that the information is traveling is always the same.

Free Hosting
Avoid free hosting. Enough said.

Seriously, if you are going to use your website for your business then you should invest in a proper hosting plan. Free hosting is often riddled with ads and popups to get people to make purchases. This is how the provider can offer you hosting for free. They are getting your website visitors to pay your bill. This can take business away from you and also hurt your reputation and image. People will classify your site as a spammy site and will be reluctant to return.

In addition, since it is free the support may not be as good. They are not working for your money so they really have no obligation to you. In some cases, they may charge for support. Thus, you'll end up paying anyway. Basically, you're better off using a real hosting provider.

Whichever type of hosting you choose, make sure to do your research. You need to know what you are getting into and how other people like the provider. Get on some Facebook groups and ask people what hosting company they use. Read some reviews and see what you think is best. In addition, make sure to consider things like website speed, price, support quality, et cetera. It may also be a good idea to find some sites that are hosted by those providers and run some analytics on them.

As long as you do your research and know what you are getting into then you'll be fine. Choose the hosting plan that you believe is right for you. You can always change it or upgrade along the way. I recommend you start out with a shared hosting account. Then you can upgrade as your website grows. Make sure you stay within your limits and things will go smoothly.

Building Your Website

After you have your domain name and web hosting, you need to build your website. This is one of the most important aspects of your affiliate marketing

Getting Set Up

business. Your website is your storefront. You are going to drive all of your traffic back to your website so it needs to be well-built. This usually means you will have to hire someone to do it for you or spend a lot of time learning how to do it yourself.

There are a number of affiliate store builders on the market that you can use to quickly set up your website. They are premade templates that you can purchase on JVZoo, Warrior Plus, or some other online vendor. You can integrate them with Amazon or other affiliate vendors and they will automatically import products for you and set up your site. In addition, you can also use plugins to help you import products. I've made a number of videos reviewing the best Amazon affiliate plugins. You can see them on my YouTube channel.

If you are going to build your website on your own then there are three main things that you need to consider. The first one is the platform you use to build your site. Are you going to use HTML, WordPress, Wix, Joomla, or something else? The second is your theme. There are many website themes available that can all provide a different look and feel for your site. The third thing you need to consider is the use of plugins. Are you going to use them? If so, which ones and how many?

Platform
The platform is how your site is built. It is the base of your site and will determine what types of themes and plugins you can use if any. Most platforms are free and easy to install directly through your hosting account CPanel. I personally like WordPress. It is one

of the most popular builders out there and is super easy to use. In addition, there are so many themes and plugins designed for it, which makes it a lot easier to accomplish what you want to accomplish.

Themes
The theme for your website dictates how all of your content is displayed. Different platforms have different themes and they are not all interchangeable. There are a number of free themes on the market. However, you will probably have better luck with a theme you purchase. This is because you are likely going to run into conflicts and will need support. If you purchase a theme, the theme creator usually provides support. On the other hand, free themes may not provide support.

Many themes have templates that you can import. These templates are often niche specific. You may be able to find the perfect template that exactly relates to the niche in which you are selling. If not, you can always import a template and customize it to fit your niche. Doing so will reduce the time it takes to design your site and also provide your website with a great modern look and feel.

Plugins
Plugins are used to do extra things on your website. Things like popups, opt-ins, contact forms, display elements, et cetera are all accomplished through the use of plugins. You can also use plugins to speed up your site, track user information, and countless other tasks.

Getting Set Up

When using plugins, you need to watch for conflicts. Often times, a plugin may conflict with your theme or another plugin. If this is the case, you may have to remove that plugin and find a different one. Or you can try to find some form of a workaround. It is also important not to use too many plugins as they can slow down your site. In addition, they can also be areas of vulnerability that open your site up to hacking attacks.

Overall, plugins are a great feature and I use many of them on my site. I highly recommend using them. Find some great plugins that help you accomplish what you need to accomplish and put them to good use. If you do your research you'll be able to make them all work properly together. If not, simply find a different plugin that works. There are tons of them out there.

If most of this last section was over your head then you will definitely want to hire a web developer to design your site for you. There are plenty of them available and you can most likely find someone on Fiverr who can quickly create a few page website for you. The main thing is that once you get your business up and running, you need to have a website. Even if you only have a landing page or splash page, something is better than nothing. Get your site live and then you can spend more time learning about it and how to make some design improvements on your own.

Most of your active promotions are going to come from social media anyway. You are going to do all of your marketing there and send people back to your blog. Thus, you will need to learn how to create blog posts on your website so that you can direct people to them through your social media accounts. This is pretty simple as long as you know how to create a post on your platform and theme.

Your Blog
Blogging is going to become your profession. Yes, you are an affiliate marketer but your blog is how you are going to sell products. You are now a marketing writer. You can't simply expect to post products and have people purchase them. No, you are going to need to tell people about the products and show them why they need to purchase them. You are now in the writing/sales and marketing business. Your goal is to find products and sell them to other people so you can earn a commission.

There are many ways you can structure your blog. Once you have the formatting down based on your website theme, you are good to go. Then, all you have to do is start creating posts about the products. You can write product reviews, tell people about your experience, make product videos, compare products, or anything you think of that will entice people to click on your affiliate link and purchase the product.

You can also use plugins to create blog posts for you on autopilot. This seems like a great thing to do because you can simply set up your site and forget about it. The trouble is, that if you forget about it then it probably isn't going to make any money for you. You need to constantly be working on it and making sure that everything is functioning properly. Your site needs to look amazing and get people to click on your

Getting Set Up

links.

Using auto-posting plugins is a great way to simplify your process. If you choose to do this, then you will definitely want to go in and edit the posts once they have gone live. Add in some of your own content and make them seem like they were entirely written by you. You can add some different stories, comparisons, experiences, et cetera. In addition, you can also expand upon the content that is already there.

These plugins will be a great help to your blog because they will retrieve all kinds of data and information that would take you a long time to gather. Many of them can get the images, details, descriptions, reviews, and more for a product and organize it nicely in a post on your website. Doing all of this yourself would take forever. Therefore, use these plugins and then go back in and add some personal touches to the post. This will help ensure that you have all of the metadata and some natural human elements to the post. Both of these things will greatly increase your website ranking.

Once you have written the blog post for the product, you'll share that post to multiple social media sites. This will drive traffic back to your website, which will greatly improve your search ranking and website statistics. In addition, it will also help establish your credibility and build your brand. Once people land on your website, they will be able to view your blog post and will be inspired to click on your affiliate link. Then, hopefully, they will purchase the product so you will receive an affiliate commission.

Start Affiliate Marketing

The main thing you need to remember is that your website is the face of your business. Therefore, it is essential that you have a great domain name, a solid hosting provider, and an amazing website. Yes, you are going to have to do some research and painstakingly find the right services to make your business work but it is worth it. You'll also have to learn how to create and post blog posts on your website. This is a pretty easy process but it can be overwhelming at first. Don't worry, you'll get better and better as time goes on. Remember, practice makes perfect.

If you set up the groundwork with a solid hosting provider then that will elevate a lot of headaches in the future. This will make running your affiliate marketing business a lot more enjoyable and significantly less stressful. I'm speaking from years of experience and countless hours of frustration. I can't say this enough, get a good hosting provider. Take the time to get your website set up and learn how to write blog posts. Schedule your auto-posting plugins and edit the posts when they go live. Share them and you will be very well set up to start receiving some traffic to your website.

Social Media

Social media is something that has been touched on all throughout this book. In addition, since you most likely already have several social media accounts and a good working knowledge of how to use them, we won't spend much time here. The main thing that you need to know is that it is very important for you to have social media accounts that are directly associated

Getting Set Up

with your affiliate marketing business. Usually, that means creating an entirely new set of accounts under your business name.

Create social media accounts on as many of the popular social media and networking sites that you feel comfortable. Facebook, Twitter, Pinterest, YouTube, Google Plus, Instagram, and Tumblr are great places to start. It is important that you use the same name, or a very similar name, so that your brand recognition will be increased. Be sure to accurately and completely fill out all of the profile details in each of the accounts.

In addition, link to all of the other accounts within each of the accounts. This way, people will be able to connect with you on any of the other platforms that they have. Another good practice is to connect with your personal account. Then, share your business accounts on your personal account so that your friends can see and support your business account.

There is so much more to social media than can be written about in this book. Each platform is a world of its own. Therefore, I encourage you to take a look at the social media books I have available. You'll find a book written specifically for many of the popular social media platforms. Remember that logistics is very important and if you have everything set up properly your life will be much easier going forward.

Start Affiliate Marketing

Chapter 4:

SEO

SEO, or Search Engine Optimization, is one of the most important aspects of your website. If you don't have your site optimized for search engines, then your content will never be found. That means you need to do everything you can to make sure that your site is optimized. Fortunately, this is pretty easy if you know what to do. Half the battle is making sure you create good content that is filled with keywords and human-written content. That means it sounds natural instead of like a robot.

If you use an auto posting plugin, then you will already have tons of keyword rich metadata. You'll also have some great images and other information that the search engine bots will be able to retrieve. Then, once you add some personal touches you'll have a great post that looks naturally written and is filled with valuable SEO information.

Unfortunately, that isn't enough to ensure that the search engine bots and web crawlers find your posts. You need to physically tell them about your posts so that they can go there and crawl them. This can be done by submitting your links to search engines, creating backlinks, indexing your links, and submitting your sitemap to search engines.

Yes, this sounds like a lot, and it is if you don't know what you are doing. You could easily spend countless hours manually tracking down all of the places to do each of these things. The trouble is that you would have no time to do anything else! Therefore, the easiest and most effective way for you to get a handle on your SEO is to create an account with Google Search Console also called Google Webmasters.

Google Search Console

Creating an account and getting everything set up can be a tiresome process. However, you'll be very glad you completed the process once it is done. Create your account and add your domain name to the console. You'll have to verify that you own it by completing one of the verification methods. Then you will have access to all kinds of great tools that you can use to rapidly boost your SEO.

Due to the fact that Google is always updating and

changing things, the instructions here will be rather generic. You'll get the idea and will have to do a little digging to find out exactly where you need to go within your property settings. The good news is that the search console is pretty easy to navigate. If you ever have trouble finding something simply run a Google search. Often times Google will take you to the exact place.

The first thing you'll want to do is submit your sitemap to Google. This can be done directly within your property, often on the home page. If it doesn't show up there look in the menu for the word "sitemaps". Then add your sitemaps there. The Yoast SEO plugin is an essential free plugin that you should have on your website if you are using WordPress. It will generate sitemap URL's for you. Simply copy them and paste them into the sitemap submission area in the Google Search Console.

The next thing you need to do is have Google index and crawl your site. Go to the area of the search console called "fetch as Google" and enter some of your web page URL's. Once the site has been fetched, then you can choose whether you want Google to index the page and links on the page. Do this with as many URL's as you can each month.

Another important task you need to complete is submitting all of your URL's to Google. Simply perform the following Google search "submit URL to Google" and then paste in each of your URL's one by one and hit submit. You can do this as many times as you like and should definitely do it each time you publish a new post. You can also do this within your search console but you'll have to complete a captcha each time.

There are many more great tools in the Google search console that you can use to help your site. Experiment with them and complete what you can. As long as you focus on the three above then you'll be in pretty good shape. However, the more you do the better your site will perform. In addition, be sure to perform each of these actions at least once a month.

Fetching your site can only be done a certain amount of times so be sure to use all of them each month to capitalize on the indexing of your site. Doing so will really help put your website on the map. Therefore, spend some time learning about the different tools in the Google Search Console and put several of them to use.

On-Page SEO

On-page SEO is the content that is within your website. It is important to remember that your website and the pages play a huge part in search engine optimization. One of the most important aspects of your website is the content that you write. If you write good, valuable, content that contains target rich keywords then your rank will greatly improve. However, it is important to make sure that these keywords appear naturally within your content rather than only in lists or headings.

In addition, if you frequently update your site with fresh content you will improve your SEO. Search engines like to promote sites that are active. If you are continually adding posts then you'll get a nice boost in the search results. Including images and video within your posts will also really help your SEO. Web crawlers like to find content that contains a variety of media. If you have multiple forms of media like text, images, and video then your site will do better than if it only has text.

The user-friendliness and speed of your website will also significantly impact your SEO. If people can move around on there and find what they need, then the search engines will see that people are surfing your site. The more pages these people visit and the longer people stay on your site the better it will perform.

In addition, the faster these pages load the better you will rank. People hate waiting for things to load. If your site can load in less than 3 seconds then that is excellent. Anything over 5 and you are going to need some help. Use GTMetrix to run a test on your site and see how it performs.

Search engines want to suggest sites that they know users will have a good experience on. If your site is terribly slow then that makes for a poor user experience. Therefore, they won't promote it. However, if it loads quickly then that means users will have a better time on your website. In that case, search engines will have no problem suggesting it to their users.

Another important factor is that your website is mobile-friendly. This will not only help build your brand because many users will only see your site on their mobile device, but it will also help your SEO. Search engines favor mobile sites because they know that the majority of the population surfs the web on a mobile device. If your site is mobile ready then the search engines will suggest it to mobile users.

Off-Page SEO

Not only does the content on your pages affect your SEO, so does the content off of your pages. This is called off-page SEO and is the content that points back to your website. These are things like social media posts, backlinks, indexing, pinging, sitemaps, and the other features of the Google Search Console. Having some good quality off page SEO can really help boost the ranking of your website.

Backlinks are probably one of the best off page SEO techniques available. The more websites that point to your URL the better it will perform. A backlink is simply another site that provides a link to your site. Anytime you hyperlink to a site you are giving that site a backlink. For example, when you share your affiliate link on your website, or on social media, you are creating a backlink for that affiliate platform.

Although social media is a form of backlink it isn't as credible as having a link on an actual website. The reason is that anything can be shared on social media whereas for you to get mentioned on someone's website takes a bit more doing. Therefore, it is regarded as a higher quality backlink. You should strive to get your links on as many places as possible.

However, keep in mind that high-quality backlinks are your ultimate goal.

When you have multiple backlinks to your site, web crawlers, bots, and spiders will see your URL all over the Internet and reason that it must be important. Then they will boost your site in the search rankings. The more places that link to your site the more authority your domain has. Thus, the higher it will rank in search engines.

In addition to creating backlinks for your site, you should also ping each of those backlinks. Pinging allows your links to be found significantly faster because it alerts the bots that your links exist. If you want to boost your traffic and ranking, then you need to make sure your links are pinged. After all, how much good can they do if you don't immediately tell people where they are located?

Once you have pinged your links you should index them with search engines. This can simply mean submitting the backlinks to search engines. This is important because then the search engine will notice your link on another person's site. That means you'll gain authority and ranking. The best way to take advantage of off page SEO is to create backlinks, ping them so they are found, then index them so search engines can follow them back to your site. This ensures they are found and crawled right away

Here are some very common questions regarding off page SEO

Start Affiliate Marketing

What is a backlink?
A Backlink is an incoming hyperlink from one web page to another website. The more backlinks you have pointing back to your site, the more popular it will be.

What is pinging?
Pinging tells search engines that your site has made an update and will get it indexed faster. When you ping backlinks, you are telling search engines to crawl the backlink page so they will find your link and follow it to your site. This builds your authority.

What is indexing?
Indexing a link is directly submitting that link to the search engines. Basically, you are handing them that information so they don't have to find it. When you index backlinks, they are found and crawled much faster. That means your URL is found and your site gains authority and rank.

What should I do for maximum results?
You should do all three for maximum results. When you build backlinks you have to wait for search engines to find and crawl them. When you ping links you point engines in the right direction so they can find and crawl them. When you index links, they are found and will be crawled right away.

There are many ways for you to build backlinks. The main thing to keep in mind is that your links need to be solid and reputable. Take advantage of guest posting and use that as a way to build backlinks to your site. Get other people to share your website posts on social

SEO

media. In addition, if you pay for backlinks, make sure you are getting them from a reputable place. Stay away from spam links and avoid simply posting your link all over different chat forums and messenger boards. Doing so could hurt your site.

Doing all of these things can greatly improve your SEO. Make sure that you consistently perform each of these actions. Do them at least once a month; shoot for each week if you can. This isn't a one-time deal. You need to constantly tell bots that your site exists and that you have new content. If you continually do this, you'll see your site ranking toward the top of page one within a few months.

Start Affiliate Marketing

Chapter 5:

Marketing & Advertising

At this point in time, you have accomplished a great deal for your business. You have selected your niche and target market. You've been approved as an affiliate on the required affiliate websites. You've chosen a domain name, set up your website, created the proper social media accounts, and taken care of your SEO. Now, it is time for you to start promoting and driving traffic to your posts and the products within.

Marketing and advertising can take on many different forms and there are several ways in which you can market your business and the products you promote. The main thing to remember is that now that you are in business for yourself, everything you do online is a form of marketing. As long as you have your business name associated with it, it is marketing. The most popular forms of marketing are video, social media, email, and content marketing.

Video Marketing

Video marketing is probably the most popular way to market products. In addition, it is also one of the most effective. People love videos because videos show them the product. People want to be shown things, not told them. With videos, they can see what the product looks like, how it works, and what someone is doing with it.

Videos are an extremely advantageous form of marketing because they have the potential to help multiple areas of your business. If you post the videos on your site then they will help your site rank higher in the search results. In addition, when people watch your videos, they will stay on your website for a longer period of time, which increases your rank. Not only that, but you can post the videos on YouTube and grow your channel, as well as your brand, to earn even more money.

Then, you can share those videos from YouTube and your website across your social media accounts. This will help boost your social media standing as long as others watch and share the videos. It also gives you some great content to post. Not only that, but it will provide you with some good social media backlinks. And if you put your website link in the video description, you'll get a deeper backlink. The social media site links to YouTube and YouTube links to your site. That's some good link juice!

A great way to use video marketing to your advantage is by creating review videos. You can purchase the products you are promoting and then create a review for them. As time goes on, and your business grows, you may be able to get vendors to send you the products for free! As with all video marketing, you need to do something different. Use your own style and make the videos original and unique. People need to love them.

One tactic you may consider is creating videos that push the products to the limits. People love watching crazy things online so if you are always coming up with new ways to destroy products and test their durability then there's a good chance your channel will do well. Be careful not to completely destroy the products though. You still want to prove that they are worth purchasing otherwise you may never make an affiliate sale. Like anything, there is a balance. Find it, and your videos will go viral and your affiliate sales will go through the roof!

Social Media Marketing

Social media has taken the world by storm. Billions of people have accounts on several networks and they are checking them regularly. It is the place with the largest captive audience. Social media is, therefore, an amazing place to market your business. Therefore, it is absolutely essential that you have a good social media presence for your business. That means you need to have an account on several social media sites. Make sure the accounts are completely optimized and regularly updated.

Marketing on social media is as simple as sharing content and engaging with other social media users. That is it. You don't need to spend any money, only some time. If you get involved by commenting on other people's posts and sharing content to different groups, boards, and pages then you'll be noticed in no time at all. That is the main thing. You need to engage with other people's posts and content. Then you'll get noticed and people will engage with your posts and content.

Make sure you are sharing valuable content and not merely posting spam comments everywhere. You need to be a valuable member of the community that contributes rather than hurts. If people appreciate you then they will be more likely to visit your site and make a purchase through your affiliate links. Not only that, but they will also be likely to share your posts, videos, or other content. This will considerably help your business because now you'll be placed in front of an entirely new audience that you couldn't have reached on your own.

Using social media massively increases your potential audience and allows you to reach countless amounts of people that you would not have reached otherwise. It is a great way to interact and engage with people and make them feel like you care. You can do so much on social media and as long as you are genuine then it will greatly help your business.

Social media is also an amazing research tool that you can use to find out exactly what your target audience may need or want. If you can find those needs and appeal to them by finding a product that meets them, you'll be in great shape. They'll love you for showing them exactly what they wanted! In addition, many of them may be highly interested in your reviews or demonstrations of products. They may wish they could test out all of those products but aren't able to. Instead, they watch your videos and live vicariously through you!

The bottom line is that social media is an amazing place that you need to be involved with to market your business. Share everything your business does on social media so that people can see and follow you. Contribute to the communities and help people out. Use your personal profiles to help promote your business content and get your friends to do the same. After a while, your business will really have a great social media presence.

Email Marketing

Email marketing is the infomercial of today. How else can you put your information directly in someone's home? You can't. Infomercials worked because they showed people products right in the comfort of their own living room. Nowadays, so many people use video streaming that TV ads are not as effective as they once were. Thus, to get in someone's home, people use email marketing.

Email is one of the most used services in today's world. It is the most used mailing service and is super effective because it's instant and free. Emails give you a way to provide great information to many people with only a few clicks. In an instant, they will have all of that information available to them right on their screen. An interesting email can inspire people to visit your site, click your affiliate links, and purchase a product.

However, there are many things to consider when using email to market your affiliate products. The first one is how you acquire the email addresses. Ideally, you should only email people that have opted into your mailing list on your website. This way you will know for certain that they will be interested in your emails. You'll have higher open rates, more clicks, and less chance of being flagged as spam.

If you don't have any emails, there are methods of obtaining them. You can scrape emails using different tools and find them based on pretty much any keyword. Thus, you can be pretty sure that they will be targeted recipients. However, you run a pretty high risk that they will flag you as spam because they didn't opt into your emails.

How you decide to obtain your emails is up to you. The best practice is to wait and grow your list by asking people to opt in. Capture the people that visit your site and see if you can get emails from your social media followers. Yes, it will take some time to grow a list, which is why you may choose to use other methods. However, having a highly targeted list will be a much more effective and responsive list than if you simply gather any emails you can.

When you decide it is time to start email marketing, you'll need to find a service. There are many free plans out there but you'll have to have your subscribers use the opt-in form that is directly associated with that service. You can also purchase some independent emailing programs that allow you to add your own subscribers. You can watch some reviews of a few of them on my YouTube channel. You'll also need to learn how to use whatever program you choose so you will be able to construct your email lists, messages, sequences, et cetera.

When sending emails you need to have an amazing subject line that will entice people to click on the email and open it. Then you'll need some great content that they'll want to read. The content needs to be powerful enough to get them to click on your link and go where you want them to go. All of this will take some research and experimentation. With practice, you'll learn what works best for you.

Content Marketing

Content marketing is a form of marketing that you will incorporate into every post. It is a very powerful way of bringing people to your site and making sure your site ranks well in search engines. Simply put, content marketing is the content that you write in your blog posts. Therefore, it is absolutely essential that you create good, valuable, and informative content.

Your blog will be automatically filled with all kinds of detailed information about each affiliate product that your auto posting plugin retrieves if you use one that is. Once you go in and edit each post, your content will get even better. If you do the proper SEO work to tell search engines and bots about your post then they will see your content and boost it for you. This is excellent content marketing.

In addition, you can also do content marketing off of your site. This is done through guest posting on other blogs or websites. Create some great content for someone else's blog and when people read it they'll be directed to your site. This is also a great way to build backlinks, by the way.

You can also do content marketing by posting in online discussions, chat forums, messenger boards, social media groups, et cetera. Anywhere you post valuable and informative content that other people will read and like is a form of content marketing. If you also place a link to your blog then you will get a good backlink as well. Therefore, get involved in some communities and start helping people out. Post valuable and informative content and include a link to your site.

One valuable thing to remember is that not all of your blog posts need to include an affiliate product. In fact, it will be very beneficial for you to periodically post regular blog posts in which you simply write text and include some pictures. Select a current trending issue that is related to your niche and write a post about it. This will generate some good interest and discussion. It will help build your brand and show people that you are not always out to make a sale.

Content marketing is the easiest form of marketing because all it takes is some time and effort. You are doing the things that you have to do anyway to build your brand and business. Therefore, remember that it is very important to be active on social media, messenger forums, chats, groups, et cetera. This will give you great awareness and recognition. Even though you may find it tedious, or like a waste of time, it is an important method for building your brand.

Advertising

Advertising is something that all businesses should do if they want to build more brand recognition and get more business. It's simple logic. The more people that see your brand the more people will know about your brand. When more people know of your brand the chances of people purchasing through you increase. Think about it. If you have the option to place your business in front of thousands of people or in front of hundreds of people which would be better? Thousands. Therefore, strongly consider doing some advertising for your business.

What type of advertising should you do? There are many different places to advertise and they all cost money, some more than others. Finding the right market can be tricky. Fortunately, it isn't as hard as

Start Affiliate Marketing

you may think and is, in reality, quite easy. You run an online business, therefore, your ads will be most beneficial on the computer. You don't want to run local TV or radio ad campaigns because by the time someone gets to the Internet they'll have forgotten your ad.

You need to run ads on the Internet. You know that people are on the Internet when they see your ad. Therefore, all they have to do is click on it for the ad to work. You need to make it easy for them to get to your site. Consider running promotions on social media networks, search engines, YouTube videos, even in apps if you can. Basically, begin by looking into all of the places you see an advertisement when you are online. Research the cost and see if it is something you can do.

Creating Ads

Creating ads is usually very simple because most advertising platforms walk you through it step-by-step. In addition, some, like Google and Bing, offer you free phone support so they'll take you through everything from start to finish while you are on the phone with them. This is huge because then you'll have an advertising expert making sure that your ads are perfectly set up to get maximum results.

When you start advertising, it is best to start with Google and Bing. These two places will put your ads in the search results and other places and only charge you when someone clicks on your ad. You'll be placed in front of thousands of people. Even if only a few hundred click, thousands saw your ad. You can also advertise on Facebook. However, keep in mind, that it could be more expensive depending on the type of campaign you run.

Facebook ads are generally more expensive than Google and Bing because Facebook can promise that your ads are highly targeted. They know that they will be able to place your ads in front of people who are definitely interested in your products. Thus, clicks may cost more. However, you may achieve higher conversion rates so it is worth experimenting with Facebook ads to see how they work for you.

You can also create video ads to place in mobile apps and on YouTube. These ads are pretty cool because you have a variety of payment options that are fairly inexpensive. Most of the time, you'll only pay when someone clicks your ad or watches the entire video ad. That means if they skip it, you're not charged but they still see your brand.

Optimizing Ads

Optimizing your ads is fairly simple especially with the step-by-step instructions on Google and Bing. What's even cooler, is that you can create your ad on Google and then import them to Bing so you don't have to do it all over again. In addition, take full advantage of the free phone support. They'll really make sure your ads are optimized.

Regarding Facebook, fill out all of the required areas and make sure you do some research on the types of ads available. You can boost posts or create your own ad campaigns. Try both of them and see which one is best for your budget. You'll probably have better luck with creating individual ad campaigns rather than boosting posts. This is because it will be more cost effective for you.

Boosting posts is a great way to get some more recognition. However, it can be expensive and the conversions generally are not very high. Therefore, when boosting posts have it in mind that it is mainly an awareness advertisement. You are paying for more people to see your ad and build your brand. Make sure you have a great image because that is most likely the only thing that they will see.

Optimizing your video ads can be a little more difficult because the best practices change on a weekly, if not daily, basis. Sometimes active video content is best and other times putting words on a screen is best. You have to do some research and see what other people are doing and who is having the most success. You'll also have to take your situation into account. Do you have the capability to create a live video with a good background and sound quality? If not, then you may be better off using a power point presentation and recording your screen while you narrate the text.

Either way, make sure your script is captivating and you use several keywords in your spoken content. This way, when the text is crawled, it will sound more natural and your ad will rank. This will help it appear on more related videos and will also help your conversion rate. Another cool trick is to tell people right away what the ad is about. Then tell them to skip the ad if they are not interested. This will help ensure that you are not paying to show your ad to someone who isn't interested in your content.

When it comes to optimizing your ads, you will have to do your research. Things are always changing, so take advantage of any free advice that the advertising platform is willing to give you. After all, they are the people who will know the most about what works and what doesn't work. You are not going to ask a Google representative about advertising on Facebook. They aren't going to have all the details. You'll ask them about Google. Capitalize on those benefits and use them to your advantage.

Remember, that running advertising campaigns takes time and money. You are probably not going to see results in a month. It will take several months. Therefore, when you start running ads, plan to run them for at least three to six months. At this point in time, you will have some good data and you'll be able to see what is working and what isn't working. You'll be able to diagnose the problem areas and fix them.

For example, if you get several clicks but no sales, then that means there must be something wrong with the content on your website. For some reason, people are not converting. The ad is doing its job of getting people to click but your web page isn't doing its job of getting people to make a purchase. Thus, you need to change the web page. You are likely going to have to restructure several things throughout the advertising process. It's kind of like trial and error. Know this ahead of time so that you will be ready to do it when the time comes.

As always, pay attention to what your competitors are doing, especially those that have a large advertising budget. If they have a large budget then they are likely trying and testing many different methods. See what they are doing and model your designs after theirs. They obviously wouldn't be spending lots of money on ads if it wasn't working for them. Therefore, the ads they are running are most likely effective. If you can model them, you'll save yourself a lot of time and money.

Chapter 6:

Building A Brand

Your brand and your business are one and the same. Your brand is the image of your business. It is what people will think of when they think of your business. You want them to see your ads, your posts, your content, et cetera and instantly think of your brand and business. You need to have good brand awareness if you are going to succeed.

Sure, you are not promoting products that are your own brand, but you still have a brand. You are an affiliate marketer and you will be identified and remembered for the content you produce. People will begin to recognize your brand and they'll know that it is the best place to go to to find great information about the products in your niche. They'll come back to you time and time again because they know they can trust your reviews, suggestions, et cetera.

Look at travel websites. Places like Hotwire, Trivago, Priceline, Kayak, Expedia, et cetera. They all have a brand and they have worked hard to build that brand. They are making fortunes selling products that are not their own. They are referring people to airline purchases, hotels, and rental cars. They sell these services for the actual companies and receive an affiliate commission on the sale.

They have done such a good job of branding that many people go to these sites instantly when booking a flight. Many people don't even book through the airlines anymore! Instead, they navigate to the booking agency of their choice and purchase their package. This is your goal when working to build a brand. You want people to visit your site to purchase products in a certain niche. You want people to trust your information and then take action based on your recommendations.

In order to achieve this, you must make sure that your information is valuable. In addition, your visitors need to be able to recognize you right away. They need to be able to instantly know who created the post, article, guest post, social media post, ad, et cetera. The best way to accomplish this is through the use of your branding material. These are things like your business name, logo, slogan, et cetera.

We've already discussed the importance of selecting a

niche-specific domain name that is easy to remember. These points transfer to everything in your business. Your logo needs to fit your niche and be easy to see and remember. It cannot be complex and must be simple. Make sure the colors stand out so that they catch people's attention and stay in their mind. Unless you are great at graphics design, you'll probably want to have someone on Fiverr design a logo for you.

Remember that your brand is everything that you do. It is much more than your name, logo, colors, et cetera. Your brand is everything you do as a business. The content you post and the things you promote are a huge representation of your brand. Therefore, always pay attention to how you conduct yourself as a business online. The more places you can post and share your content the faster you will raise awareness and build your brand.

Target Your Market

You already know who your target market is. Now you need to target your market. You know the people that are going to be interested in your products and who will, hopefully, support your business. This means you need to target them. You need to have your content designed specifically with them in mind. They need to like your brand and instantly become aware of, and remember your brand.

Your entire business revolves around these people and getting them to make purchases through your affiliate links. Therefore, everything you do, you do for them. Got it? You are not doing all of this work to make money or to get rich. You are doing all of this work to meet the needs of your target market and satisfy their demands and desires. If you can do this, then they will become loyal followers of your brand and they'll become your source of income for years to come.

The best way to continually do this is to continue to get to know your target market. Learn all you can about them. Know what they like to do, what they eat, their political stance, religion, family values, et cetera. If you can learn all of these things and then tailor your content to agree with their values then you'll be all set. You need to be like a politician in this regard. Your goal is to wine and dine, to schmooze, you need to woo them.

Therefore, get involved where they are involved. Spend time in the chat rooms and online forums. Post on social media, write helpful comments, and create content that you know they will enjoy. If you can do this, you'll be an amazing affiliate marketer and your brand will rapidly grow. You'll gain tons of loyal followers who will be happy to support you by making purchases through your affiliate links.

Your Voice

The best brands are business that people can really relate to. They feel like the brand is speaking directly to them. They feel like they can look inside and see what they want. These are the brands that know their customers and know how to speak directly to them. They speak in such a way that they are addressing millions yet it feels like they are talking one-on-one. People see these brands as a person rather than a business.

Your goal is to achieve this status. You need to be seen as a person even though you are a brand. This is pretty easy to accomplish because if you show your visitors that you care then you will be seen as a person. Businesses are typically thought of as machines. They are a business, there is no heart, they don't care, and their purpose is to make money. People have hearts, they can care, and they can do things for others. If you build your brand so it seems like it is a person then people will love you.

Your visitors aren't looking for ads that tell them about items. They want to be shown the item. They want to see how it is going to help them and make their lives better. You need to appeal to their selfish nature by becoming selfless. Show your visitors that your business cares about them. Your brand voice needs to convey that sense of love, security, and thoughtfulness. Don't worry about being "professional" be a human being.

If you continually add a human element to your brand, then people will see that you are a human. Of course, you are a human and they need to think of you as a human, not a business machine. They need to be able to connect with you and should be able to consider your advice like they consider the advice of a friend. If you speak to them in humanistic terms and talk in a way that seems like you are talking directly to them, then your voice will really help you build your brand.

Your voice is instantly visible wherever you write content. It will be on your website, in your social media posts, your discussions, and anywhere you write content online. It is important to maintain the same voice and writing style throughout all of your content. You don't want to have some writing be detailed and analytical and then other content be sarcastic. You need to maintain the same level of tone, humor, and poise throughout all of your writing.

The better you know your audience, the better you will be able to speak to them. Therefore, strive to learn all you can about them so that you can effectively communicate to them and with them. If you can speak in a way that makes them feel like you are speaking directly to them, then you will have no trouble at all building a loyal following for your brand.

Visual Branding

Your visual brand is something that helps tie everything together. It is the glue that helps people associate your voice, content, et cetera to your business. Your visual brand consists of things like your logo, website colors, featured images, typography, et cetera. It is the things that people see and remember not read and remember.

When designing your visual brand, it is important that you create everything so that your target market will like it. This means selecting colors and fonts that you know they will enjoy. Once again, the better you know your target market the easier this will be.

Building A Brand

Create designs that will appeal to them based on your knowledge of them.

You can also create several different designs and then reach out to your audience asking them to vote on their favorite design. This is a great way to make your audience feel important and show them that you value their opinion. It will also help ensure that you use designs that you know they'll like.

Visual branding is a large part of your brand and you need to make sure that you are creating designs that appeal to your viewers. Like everything you do, you are doing it for them. You may not personally like the way it looks, but as long as they like it then that is fine. Remember that you are working to serve your audience. They are the people that will make your business possible. Be good to them and they'll be good to you.

Brand Consistency

Brand consistency is another very important aspect when it comes to building your brand. If you have all kinds of different components compiled together you will have a lot of trouble getting people to recognize your brand. You need to be consistent across all areas of your business. This not only means being consistent across multiple different platforms, it also means being consistent across different branding areas.

The different areas of your brand like your voice, logo, colors, images, et cetera should all have a cohesive look and feel. Everything should flow together and look like it belongs. You want them to complement and accent each other so that together they are better than if they are separate. Achieving this usually means hiring a web developer or getting some consultation on your design from a professional.

It's also important that you are consistent across multiple platforms. This not only applies to your voice, as mentioned earlier, it applies to everything you do. If you have your logo as your business profile picture on Facebook then you should have your logo as your profile picture on Twitter and all other social media sites as well. In addition, your header images should be the same on each platform. Consistency is key. You are building a brand not a collection of modern art.

Keeping everything the same will not only make your life easier, it will also help people recognize and associate your brand and business. It prevents a lot of confusion and people will always be able to know exactly whose profile they are visiting.

Chapter 7:

Stick With It

Affiliate marketing is an amazing way for you to earn a passive income. You can set up your business and it will become your retirement program. What's even more exciting is that it can also be an inheritance for future generations. As long as you continue to get visitors and clicks you'll continue to receive affiliate commissions year after year.

Remember, this isn't going to be easy. Building a successful affiliate marketing business takes hard work and determination. It is like building any business. You will need to put in a lot of hours before you start seeing real payouts. The good thing about affiliate marketing businesses is that the overhead is relatively low. For many months you may only make a double-digit income. It could even be a few years!

It will all depend on how quickly you accomplish tasks and get your business set up. The faster you get things done the better chance you'll have. This doesn't mean getting it done haphazardly. You need to do it right. Therefore, take however much time it takes. Some things will take longer than others. Keep working at it and you will succeed.

Work hard to keep yourself from buying into the "get rich quick" mentality. Focus on your goals and keep working. Many people out there claim that you can make tons of money by doing little to no work at all. This is very far from the truth. Everything takes work and you cannot expect to make money by doing nothing. Stay the course and don't flip-flop from one thing to another. Doing so will be very counter-productive.

For example, let's say that building a successful business of any kind will take 5 years to make a good income. Now, if you focus on one business for 5 years then you'll start making your living from that one business. However, if you work on it for a few years and then decide to try something else for a year, then something else, then go back to the original plan, you'll be five years in and still won't be making a living.

This is a simple example but it makes the point. You need to stay focused on what you start. See it through and keep working. If you do your research and continually make sure you are keeping up with the current trends then you'll do very well. It doesn't happen overnight. So be ready to roll up your sleeves and get to work.

If you are looking for a business opportunity that will make you a millionaire in a matter of weeks then, unfortunately, affiliate marketing is not for you. However, if you are looking for an opportunity to make money by growing a business from scratch with very little start-up money and a large initial time investment then this is exactly what you want.

Make a Commitment

If you are going to build a successful affiliate marketing business then you are going to need to make a commitment. You need to be driven to accomplish certain things each day or week. You must set goals. You have to be willing to designate a few hours each day to build your business. This means working some late nights and potentially weekends without seeing any immediate returns.

One of the great things about this business is that you don't need to commit a lot of money. You can get started with very little, or even nothing at all. However, it is best if you can dedicate $50, or so, a month. This is nothing for a business start-up. Nothing. What affiliate marketing lacks in monetary startup costs it makes up for in time commitment. You'll need to dedicate lots of time to get things going.

Of course, if you have lots of money and little time then you could hire someone to do all of this for you.

Start Affiliate Marketing

Then you would be committing large amounts of money and very little time. Either way, you will have to commit to making your business a success.

Stay Up To Date

The Internet is an ever-changing place. Because of this, affiliate marketing is always changing. You need to be constantly aware of the changes on the Internet. This sounds a lot harder than it really is. Basically, all you need to pay attention to are any policy updates on any of the affiliate marketing platforms you are signed up with. In addition, watch out for any SEO algorithm changes that could affect your performance.

Of course, you'll need to stay up to date with the latest products and trends within your niche and all of the other normal business updates. However, these things you'll do regularly without thinking about them. The areas you need to really watch out for are changes in SEO algorithms and policy updates, which will most likely be emailed to you. However, if you miss things in those areas you could miss out on some business.

You'll also want to be consistently updating and maintaining your website and social media profiles. Your website is not simply a set and forget system. You need to be actively creating new and relevant content so that people will find your site and purchase products through your affiliate links. You'll also want to pay attention to your current content. If products ever become discontinued or unavailable for sale you'll want to update that on your website. You should still

Stick With It

keep the posts to maintain SEO but add a note about the changes to inform your readers.

Make sure to watch out for special promotions and affiliate tools offered by the affiliate platforms. A lot of times they will give you many great resources. Obviously, they want you to succeed because it is free advertising for them. Not only is it free, it is also word-of-mouth advertising, which is very valuable for them. They know that they can make more sales when people tell other people about their products.

Therefore, do your best to stay up to date with the constantly changing Internet environment. Maintain your blog and social media profiles and continue to put out great content. After a while, you'll start getting more and more followers. Eventually, those followers will convert to sales and you'll begin making your first affiliate commissions.

If you keep at it, and diligently work hard, you will soon see some greater affiliate commissions. Perhaps a few years down the road you'll be making enough to hire some freelancers to do some of your work for you. You may even be able to find a service to help automate some things. At this point, you are one step closer to achieving a passive income.

As the years go by and you start earning even more commissions, you'll be able to step back and let other people manage things for you. At this point in time, your income will be truly passive. It may take years to get here, but it will be worth it. You'll be making money while you sleep. Not only will this be a great retirement program for you, it will be there for your children and future generations as well. If they maintain it, that is.

Chapter 8:

Conclusion

Being an affiliate marketer is not something that you do on a whim. It is a plan that you make and execute with grit and determination. It is not an overnight sensation or some viral business in a box. Affiliate marketing is a business; it's a good business that you can create over time. You can use it to provide you and your family with income for years to come. It is something that you have to want to do.

A successful affiliate marketer understands that there is much more affiliate marketing than making money. In addition, there is much more than merely promoting other people's products. A successful affiliate marketer knows that the main goal of the

Start Affiliate Marketing

business is to provide a service. If you can provide value to your visitors then they will support you by making a purchase. They are not simply going to buy because you want them to buy. They will only buy if they want to buy.

In order for you to excel in the world of affiliate marketing, you need to build an amazing brand. You need to reach your audience with a wide variety of tools such as video, blog posts, social media, emails, et cetera. Use as many marketing methods as you can and really put yourself out there. Don't count on being found. Instead, place yourself in front of people so they run into you. This is how you will be found online.

Hopefully, by now, you have a pretty good understanding of what you need to do to become a successful affiliate marketer. You need to choose your niche, become an affiliate, build a website, and start marketing to build your brand. It's up to you to use this information to fuel your desires of becoming the best affiliate marketer that you can be.

No matter your experience level, how much money you have, how much time you have, et cetera you can be successful. All it takes is the desire. If you make the commitment to be a successful affiliate marketer then you will become a successful affiliate marketer. Therefore, make your business plan and get started. Set some goals, put in the time, and you'll reap what you sow. Eventually, you'll have a great affiliate marketing business that will pay you for years to come.

Appendix:

Resources

Best Amazon Affiliate Plugins
https://www.youtube.com/watch?v=CObZpOTJleI&list=PLGsUva4ceGvE7QTSU0BU8H3YBlIQzJ5Ra

Email Program Reviews
https://www.youtube.com/watch?v=pPKzFLbov4E&list=PLGsUva4ceGvFeh5QiE3O103IbJXgLfrOz

Sell My eBooks and Get 100%
https://spencercoffman.com/become-an-affiliate

Start Affiliate Marketing

About The Author

Affiliate Marketing is second nature for Spencer Coffman. He's always promoting something, selling something, and looking for a deal. He's gone through and tested several affiliate marketing programs, software programs, plugins, et cetera. Spencer knows that the foundation is the most important aspect of any business, especially an affiliate marketing business. That's why he's dedicated so much time to researching the best tools for the job. This book will show you exactly how to build your affiliate marketing business from the ground up. Get started today! To read more about Spencer, visit his website spencercoffman.com

Start Affiliate Marketing

About The Author

Start Affiliate Marketing

www.ingramcontent.com/pod-product-compliance
Lightning Source LLC
Chambersburg PA
CBHW071747240526
45471CB00022B/607